The SPORTS HEROES Library

WINNING WOMEN of Tennis

Nathan Aaseng

Lerner Publications Company • Minneapolis

ACKNOWLEDGMENTS: The photographs are reproduced through the courtesy of: p. 4, Russ Adams Productions, Inc.; pp. 8, 13, 19, 21, 22, 24, 29, 32, 37, 41, 44, 48, 50, 52, 54, 61, 62, 64, 69, 70, 73, 78, 79, Wide World Photos, Inc.

Cover photograph: Russ Adams Productions, Inc.

To Joan, the expert

LIBRARY OF CONGRESS CATALOGING IN PUBLICATION DATA

Aaseng, Nathan.
  Winning women of tennis.

  (The Sports heroes library)
  SUMMARY: Brief biographies of eight famous women on the international tennis scene including Helen Wills, Althea Gibson, Margaret Smith Court, Billie Jean King, Chris Evert Lloyd, Evonne Goolagong, Martina Navratilova, and Tracy Austin.

  1. Women tennis players — Biography — Juvenile literature [1. Women tennis players. 2. Tennis players] I. Title. II. Series: Sports heroes library.

  GV994.A1A174   796.342′092′2 [B] [920]   81-6033
  ISBN 0-8225-1067-7   AACR2

Manufactured in the United States of America

International Standard Book Number: 0-8225-1067-7
Library of Congress Catalog Card Number: 81-6033

1 2 3 4 5 6 7 8 9 10 90 89 88 87 86 85 84 83 82 81

Contents

Chris Evert Lloyd, four-time winner of the U.S. Open, congratulates her opponent, Tracy Austin, on Austin winning her first Open title in 1979.

Introduction

"Sphairistike, anyone?" If Major Walter Clopton Wingfield had been granted his wish, the popular game of tennis would have been called "sphairistike."

In the 1870s, Major Wingfield observed that people were growing more interested in outdoor recreation. He also noticed that there were almost no accepted sports for women. Other than swimming and badminton, there was not much that a woman could do for exercise.

In 1874 the major took advantage of the situation. He borrowed some ideas from the racquet games that had been played in England since the 1400s and invented a new game. Wingfield patented his ball and racquet game under the name *sphairistike*, the Greek word for "playing ball." Sphairistike was to be played outdoors by both men and women. With its high net and narrow court, the game resembled badminton in many ways.

Sphairistike caught on quickly, or at least the idea did. But poor Major Wingfield soon had trouble recognizing the game he had started. In a period of only five years, people had changed Wingfield's rules and were playing the sport by the rules that exist today. The awkward name "sphairistike" never caught on either, and the game became known as tennis.

The new game of tennis soon spread to other parts of the world. In 1874, the same year it was invented, it was introduced in the United States. Mary Ewing Outerbridge, an American sportswoman, purchased some tennis equipment from British army officers in Bermuda. After bringing this equipment back to the United States, Outerbridge set up the first United States tennis courts on the grounds of the Staten Island Cricket and Baseball Club in New York City.

Meanwhile in England, tennis received its first major boost from the Wimbledon Croquet Club when one of their carefully groomed grass croquet lawns was changed into a tennis court. In 1877 Wimbledon became the setting for the first major tennis tournament. And today, more than one hundred years later, Wimbledon is still where the top tennis tournament in the world is held. And the courts are still grass that has been grown and cut to make a smooth playing surface.

Along with Wimbledon, three other tennis tournaments make up what is known as the Grand Slam: the French, the United States, and the Australian opens. One of the most impressive feats in tennis today is to win all four in one year.

Because it began in high society in England, for many years tennis was only for the privileged. Exclusive tennis clubs and strict dress codes helped to keep the average person off the courts. And although women were allowed to play, at that time the thought of paying women to play tennis or, in fact, any sport seemed foolish. As late as the 1950s, American tennis star Althea Gibson was forced to give up the game in search of a better living.

It was not until the 1970s that changes really started to take place in the sports world. Women were demanding recognition and equal opportunities, and it was the women tennis players who led the fight. Through the efforts of stars such as Billie Jean King, women were finally finding a respected place for themselves in athletics.

Today women tennis players are genuine sports stars. They have become as popular and as successful as their male counterparts in the game. The eight women in this book are among the top women tennis players in the world, and they have done much to bring about the success that women's tennis enjoys today.

Helen Wills reaches high but misses a ball in the 1935 finals at Wimbledon. She went on to win the match.

1
Helen
Wills

The 1920s was the decade of sports heroes. Babe Ruth was swatting home runs in record numbers. Jack Dempsey and Gene Tunney were battling each other toe to toe in the boxing ring. Red Grange, "The Galloping Ghost," was turning football into a national craze. With all of this activity in other sports, no one was paying much attention to tennis.

But in 1926, tennis suddenly grabbed the sports headlines. Even people who did not know a tennis racquet from a fly swatter were talking about the big match between Suzanne Lenglen and Helen Wills. That contest would be the first singles match between the world's two top women players. Lenglen, a polished French tennis artist, had won the women's singles title at Wimbledon in 1920, 1921, 1922, 1923, and 1925. And Wills, a young Californian, was beginning to look just as good after winning three straight U.S. Open titles in 1923, 1924, and 1925.

Although the match promised to be one of the best in years, the conditions were hardly ideal. The French court was tucked between some ratty-looking buildings and had poor facilities. Yet seats were selling for $11 each, an unheard-of price in those days. That amount was six times more expensive than a ticket to the famous Wimbledon matches.

But none of those problems seemed to matter, and people rushed to the courts on the day of the match. During the game, the tension was so high that the crowd would not give the players the usual respectful silence. Several times Suzanne Lenglen had to ask the shouting, cheering crowd to be quiet.

As the match progressed, Lenglen and Wills played cautiously. They seldom rushed the net but instead stood back and traded their hardest shots. Lenglen finally won the first set, 6-3, but she seemed a little disturbed that the young Wills was putting up such a good fight. In the second set, Wills scrambled for all she was worth and managed to lead most of the way. But near the end, Wills was stunned by a questionable call that seemed to break her concentration. Wills lost the set, 6-8, and Lenglen won the match. It had been a long, hard-fought match that had left both players gasping for breath. Even hours after the match, Suzanne Lenglen was still so winded she could barely speak.

Helen Wills was a loser that day, but it was a rare loss. Her brave struggle against the more experienced champ had toughened her up for the years ahead. The very next year, Wills went to Wimbledon and won. That win was the beginning of an incredible streak, and from 1927 to 1938, Wills never lost any Wimbledon contests.

Helen Wills was born in Centerville, California, in 1906. When she was growing up, her best friend had been a boy who played tennis all the time. Helen decided that if she wanted to be with him, she had better learn the game. Another one of Helen's first tennis partners had been her father, who was such an excellent player that Helen always lost when she played him. Helen, in fact, did not beat her father until she was 14. But by then she could beat almost everyone else, too.

In 1921 when she was 15, Helen won the national girls' title. The next year, although she was just 16 years old, Helen entered the national tournament for women (now called the United States Open) and made it all the way to the finals before losing, 3-6, 1-6, to United States player Molla Mallory. Mallory had also won the women's singles title in 1920 and 1921. But the next year, 1923, Wills got quick revenge and stunned Mallory in the finals by the lopsided score of 6-2, 6-1. In 1924 Wills defended her title by again defeating Mallory, 6-1, 6-2.

Wills' two victories against Mallory in the 1923 and the 1924 U.S. opens had been an early warning that the coming years would be miserable ones for her opponents. During her amazing tennis career, Helen won the U.S. Open seven times—every year she entered the tournament between 1923 and 1931. (She did not play in 1926 and 1930.)

From 1927 to 1938, Wills also played in eight tournaments at Wimbledon, and she won them all. During those years, many fans were disappointed that Helen didn't enter every Wimbledon tournament—she had missed in 1931, 1934, 1936, and 1937—but rivals such as Molla Mallory, Helen Hull Jacobs, and Dorothy Round must have been grateful. When Helen wasn't playing, these stars had a much better chance of winning! Fellow North American player Jacobs, for instance, had been defeated by Wills at Wimbledon in 1929, 1932, and 1935, but she won in 1936 when Wills did not play. Jacobs had also been defeated by Wills in the 1928 U.S. Open, but she won in 1932, 1933, 1934, and 1935 when Wills was not in the tournament.

Helen Wills was also the only American woman to win an Olympic gold medal in tennis. No one knows how many Olympic gold medals she would have won because tennis was dropped from the Olympics after Helen's victory in the 1924 Games.

Throughout her career, Wills proved to be a hard

Wearing her "daring" tennis dress, Wills won her sixth singles title at Wimbledon in 1933.

player to beat. She was always on the attack and would pin down her opponents with incredibly hard shots. If Wills, or "Little Miss Poker Face" as she was called, had a weakness, no one was able to find it. The most frustrating thing for Helen's opponents was that they could rarely hit a ball out of her reach because she covered the court so well.

Besides receiving attention because of her playing, Wills created a fuss by the clothes she wore on the court. When Helen was playing tennis, a woman was expected to play in a long dress, high stockings, and long sleeves. But Helen showed up for matches in sleeveless and much shorter dresses. Wills gave this new style credit for improving women's tennis. Free from the burden of layers of clothing, women could now move about and swing their racquets much more easily. While Wills' "daring" outfit would seem uncomfortably bulky today, at that time tennis officials thought Helen's dress was most unladylike.

Although Helen was a remarkably successful player, she never earned a penny from her tennis skill. During her playing years, she preferred to remain an amateur rather than take money for playing. She reasoned that as an amateur she could play for fun. But if she were to turn pro, she would have to consider the game her life's work.

In spite of her heavy playing schedule, tennis was far from the most important thing in Helen's life. She always considered her studies more important than tennis practice. Once when she was asked which of her trophies and prizes she valued the most, she replied that it was the Phi Beta Kappa key she had earned for academic excellence in college.

Helen retired in 1938 after winning her eighth singles title at Wimbledon. She settled in California and spent much of her time raising show dogs. While her fans were disappointed, her opponents must have been glad when this amazing athlete finally quit her "hobby" of winning world championships!

2
Althea Gibson

Althea Gibson hated school. At the age of 12, she skipped classes every chance she got and roamed the streets of Harlem, New York. Althea was a sullen, bitter girl who seemed to have little chance of ever escaping from the Harlem slums. But Althea Gibson surprised the world and became America's top female athlete.

Althea was born in 1927 in a place few people have ever heard of—Silver, South Carolina. Only 50 people called Silver "home," and it wasn't much of a home at that. Althea's parents, like most of the people who lived in Silver, were sharecroppers who helped to farm land they did not own. Even in the best years, the Gibsons were barely able to grow enough to eat. Life in Silver, South Carolina, was so hard that two-year-old Althea was sent to live with her aunt in Harlem, New York. Meanwhile,

Althea's family stayed in Silver until they could save enough money to join her.

Life in Harlem, however, did not seem much better. When school was out for the summer, there was little to do, and Althea could have easily gotten into trouble. But instead she participated in a summer paddleball program. During the summer months, the Harlem Recreation Department would block off a street from traffic and set up paddleball courts. Since paddleball needed only a small space and little equipment, it was an inexpensive sport for many Harlem youngsters. Althea spent most of her time on these courts, and she soon became a talented player.

Buddy Walker, a man who worked for the recreational department, often watched Althea play paddleball. He thought she would also be great at tennis because tennis was quite similar to paddleball. So he bought Althea two used tennis racquets and turned her loose on a tennis court.

Buddy Walker was the first of many friendly people who helped Gibson in her career. It was the combined efforts of many people that made it possible for Althea to become a great tennis star.

Early in her career, Althea's main problem was not having the chance to play many of the better players. That was because few courts were open to black players then. Realizing that Gibson needed a break in order to develop her promising talents, a sympathetic tennis club chipped in and bought her a membership.

At first Althea's new friends were embarrassed by her manners. Gibson simply was not used to the ways of organized tennis. When another ball was hit into her court, Althea did not go out of her way to return it. Sometimes she even got angry at players for not keeping the ball out of her way. Often rather than congratulate an opponent for a good shot, Althea would scold herself for not doing better. And if someone beat her, Althea was usually too upset to shake hands with the winner.

But Gibson's skill and competitive nature outshone her manners. Althea soon caught the attention of Robert Johnson and Hubert Eaton, two black medical doctors who loved the sport of tennis and wanted to help black players become experts. They watched 5-foot, 11-inch, 145-pound Althea overpowering her foes on the court and decided with the proper training she would surely be a great tennis player.

The doctors soon came up with a plan for Althea. They suggested she spend her summers with Dr. Johnson to study tennis. Then during the school year, she could live with Dr. Eaton, where she would go to school and also continue to play tennis. The offer was good only if Gibson would agree to settle down and do well in school.

The offer was too good to pass up, so Althea accepted it. She settled down to a more disciplined life and studied hard both at school and on the tennis court. By 1949 Althea had graduated from high school. And by that time, she had also won every tennis championship that a young black woman could win. Althea's efforts paid off and earned her an athletic scholarship to Florida A&M University in Tallahassee.

At Florida A&M, Althea continued to blast her opponents off the courts, and it became increasingly difficult for the whites-only clubs to ignore her. Many people began saying that Gibson should be allowed to play in the national championships at Forest Hills, where no blacks had ever before played.

It was not easy to break through the color barrier. But in 1950, Althea was finally admitted to the tournament at Forest Hills. On the day of the tournament, a crowd gathered to see how Gibson would do. Some were hoping that Althea's playing would prove she did not belong there.

It must have been a lonely and scary experience for Gibson to be playing at Forest Hills. But in spite of all of the tension, Althea won her first match. In the second round, she played against one of the top U.S. players, Louise Brough. Brough had won the women's singles at the U.S. Open in 1947 and at Wimbledon in 1948, 1949, and 1950. Gibson got

Although Althea Gibson lost to champion Louise Brough in their 1950 Forest Hills match, everyone was impressed with Gibson's fine performance at her first national tournament.

off to a shaky start and lost the first set, 1-6. But in the second set, she fought back with a solid 6-3 win. In the final set, Gibson's booming drives had Brough on the run. Leading 7-6, Althea needed only one more game to win. And it looked like she would because Brough seemed to have been worn out by Gibson's power game.

But suddenly the thunder crashed, rain swept over the court, and the match had to be halted until the next day. By then a well-rested Louise Brough had regained her confidence, and she went on to win the match. But everyone felt that Althea Gibson had played an amazing first tournament.

19

After graduating from college in 1954, Althea took a job as a physical education instructor in Missouri and continued playing on the tennis circuit. Remembering her match with Brough, fans expected Gibson to start winning tournaments right away. But Althea's playing seemed to be getting worse instead of better. It had been five years since she had lost to Brough, and Gibson still hadn't won a major tournament. Althea was ready to hang up her tennis racquet, and she considered making use of her fine singing voice and starting a concert career instead.

In 1955, while still uncertain about her future, Althea was asked to go on a world goodwill tour with a group of U.S. tennis players. Deciding that this would be a good way to end her career, Gibson joined the tour. But while she was traveling, Althea suddenly found her old competitive edge. In just eight months, she entered 18 tournaments and won 16 of them, including a 6-0, 12-10 win at the important French Open in 1956.

Althea figured that now was no time to quit. And she was right. Two years later, in 1957, she won the women's singles at Wimbledon, beating Darlene Hard of California, 6-3, 6-2. Proving that this win was no fluke, she and her partner, Darlene Hard, also took home a trophy for winning the women's doubles, 6-1, 6-2.

Gibson returns a serve to Darlene Hard at the 1957 Wimbledon finals.

Darlene Hard congratulates winner Althea Gibson at Wimbledon in 1957.

That same year, Gibson also made it to the finals of the U.S. Open. And her opponent waiting across the net was none other than Louise Brough. But this time not even a thunderstorm would have kept Althea from the title! She won the match with ease, 6-3, 6-2.

In 1958 Althea repeated her singles and doubles wins at Wimbledon. And for her efforts, she was named Female Athlete of the Year both years.

Today a top woman tennis player like Althea Gibson can win over half a million dollars in a year. But in 1958 there was little money in women's tennis, so Althea decided to put her athletic talents to another test—golf. Although she was just a beginner at the game, Althea joined the pro golf tour. Fortunately for the golfers, she was not as overpowering in golf as she had been in tennis. Still, she managed to tie for first place in an Ohio tournament in 1971.

Although she participated in two major sports, Althea Gibson will be remembered more for her achievements in tennis. When people mention her name, they think back to that day in 1950 when a lonely black girl showed she could play great tennis in the face of tremendous pressure.

At the 1965 Wimbledon finals, Margaret Smith makes a low back-hand return to defending champion, Maria Bueno.

3
Margaret Smith Court

Margaret Smith Court made an awful nuisance of herself when she was young. But because she did, she became one of the top women tennis players in history. In fact, she won far more major tennis titles than anyone else, man or woman.

Margaret Smith was born in 1941 in Albury, Australia. Tennis was a popular sport in Australia, and most of the country's top players had begun playing with the encouragement of their tennis-playing parents. But Margaret's parents did not play tennis, so it was fortunate that she lived across the street from a tennis club.

Margaret did not belong to the tennis club, but she certainly was not shy about using their courts! Margaret and the boys she ran around with found they could sneak on to one particular court hidden from view of the clubhouse. The group found no one would notice them as long as they kept the ball from straying out of the court.

Margaret's job was to play very near to the net so she could intercept the ball before it went wide. In later years, Margaret claimed this was one of the reasons she always volleyed so well as a pro. (Volleying is when a player approaches the net and returns the ball before it bounces.) Despite her best efforts, however, the ball sometimes got away from Margaret and rolled in sight of the caretaker. For a while, the caretaker spent a lot of time chasing Margaret and her friends away. Finally, he got tired of battling them, and he even offered to give Margaret tennis lessons.

As Margaret began her tennis career, it was obvious that she would need to work hard if she wanted to become a top tennis player. At first she was an awkward player, as well as being a basically shy and nervous person on the court. Some experts feel Margaret's awkwardness in her early matches was because she was left-handed but had been taught to play tennis right-handed.

To top these problems, Margaret was very frail. In order to build herself up, Margaret's coaches had her lifting weights. At first Margaret was not too thrilled with her exercise program and felt by lifting 150-pound weights, she would end up looking like a muscle-bound man. But as she grew stronger, her tennis improved, and she was glad she followed her coaches' advice.

As part of her training, Margaret also took to the roads to improve her running speed and endurance. She became such a swift runner that many urged her to try for the Australian Olympic team. It is likely she could have made the team in the 200-meter race, but she preferred tennis.

Once she began winning, Margaret moved up quickly in the ranks. In 1958, when she was only 17 years old, she took the first in a long line of Australian championships. Then in 1962 she added the United States title by beating Darlene Hard, 9-7, 6-4. The following year, she defeated Billie Jean Moffitt (King), 8-6, 7-5, at Wimbledon.

As Margaret's career progressed, she no longer looked like the frail girl she used to be. At 5 feet, 9 inches, and 150 pounds, she showed tremendous strength. In fact, a researcher found Margaret's strength to be equal to that of the average male college athlete. That information came as no surprise to the women who tried to return Smith's blistering forehands and backhands. Besides being tall, Margaret also had long arms to help her reach balls that would normally have been impossible to get. Her only shortcoming was that she sometimes wilted under pressure.

While Smith continued to win victory after victory,

her successes could not keep her from becoming unhappy with her life. Because of her basic shyness, Margaret never was close to the other players, and tennis was a very lonely life for her. In 1965, after easily sweeping both Wimbledon (against Maria Bueno, 6-4, 7-5) and the U.S. Open, (against Billie Jean Moffitt, 8-6, 7-5), Margaret quit the game and returned to Australia. There she worked in a dress shop and started dating Barry Court, a wool dealer.

Later Barry Court and Margaret Smith married, and Barry encouraged Margaret to have another try at tennis. So in 1967 Margaret returned to action. The two-year layoff had rusted her skills more than she had realized, and it took almost a year of steady practice before she again felt comfortable against the top players. But she did win the U.S. Open in 1969.

By 1970 Margaret Court was in top form, and she decided to go after the Grand Slam. Only one other woman, Maureen Connelly, had ever won the French, the U.S., and the Australian opens and Wimbledon in the same year. And that had been in 1953, almost 20 years earlier.

That year Margaret practically owned the Australian Open, and she won easily against Kerry Melville in the finals, 6-3, 6-1. In the French Open, she fought off American Rosemary Casals to win, two sets to one. Only Wimbledon and the U.S. Open remained.

Margaret Court faced three-time Wimbledon singles winner, Billie Jean King, in the 1970 Wimbledon finals.

At Wimbledon Margaret met her chief rival, Billie Jean King, in the finals. The two were so evenly matched that it seemed they would be playing forever without either gaining the upper hand.

In tennis the first person to win six games wins the set — *if* she or he wins by at least two games. At that time, there were no special rules to break ties, so Margaret and Billie Jean had to play until someone won the set by two games. In the longest final in Wimbledon history, Margaret hung on to win, 14-12, 11-9. Following that narrow escape, Margaret won the U.S. title. The Grand Slam was hers!

The next year, 1971, Margaret retired for a second time to have a baby boy, Danny. But before long, she was back in action. Although she did not consider herself to be a strong supporter of women's rights, Court's lifestyle was a little ahead of the times. During the tour, Barry took care of Danny while Margaret went out to earn money.

Margaret Court was the leading woman money winner in tennis in the early 1970s. And only one person kept her from finishing her career in glory: Bobby Riggs. Bobby Riggs was an old tennis pro who had won the U.S. Open men's singles in 1939 and 1941 and at Wimbledon in 1939 and also the 1939 Wimbledon mixed doubles (with Alice Marble). He was going around making fun of women's tennis. He boasted that, at age 55, he could easily beat the best women players. At first Margaret tried to ignore his remarks, but she finally felt forced to take Riggs up on his challenge. Because she was considered to be the best woman tennis player, it seemed up to her to uphold the reputation of women tennis players. So a match was set for May 13, 1973.

Court, unfortunately, had her worst day ever in the Riggs match. Bothered by the distracting crowd and Bobby's slow-motion game of lobs and trick shots, Margaret made countless mistakes. The match was a very brief disaster, and Court lost badly, 2-6, 1-6.

Losing to Bobby Riggs was not the climax of Margaret Court's career, however, and in 1975 Margaret won a championship in doubles at the U.S. Open. On that happy note, Court decided to retire, this time for good. Margaret and her family settled down in Perth, Australia, to spend their time sailing and raising sheep.

Margaret always thought first of herself as a family person. But that certainly didn't keep her from enjoying astounding success on the tennis court. In her career, Margaret Smith Court won 61 major titles—no one else has won even 40—and a place as one of the great women of tennis.

Billie Jean King returns a serve to Evonne Goolagong at the 1974 U.S. Open in Forest Hills, New York.

4
Billie Jean King

It seemed more like a Hollywood production than a tennis match. First a woman was carried into the stadium on a richly decorated cot. Then an older man followed, escorted by show girls. Over 30,000 people had swarmed into the Houston Astrodome to watch the "battle of the sexes," a tennis match between Billie Jean King and Bobby Riggs. As it turned out, the match was fairly dull. But it did more for tennis—especially for women's tennis—than any other match ever before played. But long before her 1973 match with Riggs, Billie Jean King had been a leading spokesperson for women's tennis —and one of the top women players in history.

Billie Jean Moffitt was born in Long Beach, California, in 1943. From an early age, Billie, or "Sis" as her family called her, showed signs of being a superior athlete. But no one was surprised, because athletic skill ran in her family. Billie Jean's father was very athletic, and her younger brother, Randy, became a pitcher for the San Francisco Giants.

In grade school, Billie Jean was usually the biggest kid, and she could always outrun the boys. She loved softball, track, and basketball and even played football. In one football game, Billie Jean kicked a field goal half the length of the field to pull out a last-second victory.

As Billie Jean grew older, her parents worried about her playing such rough games. They told her there were three sports for women: golf, tennis, and swimming. Golf and swimming didn't really interest Billie Jean, but she agreed to give tennis a try. And it didn't take 11-year-old Billie Jean long to find out that she loved tennis. In fact, she enjoyed tennis so much she wanted to drop the piano lessons she had started just six months before. But Billie Jean was told, "No piano, no tennis."

In every spare moment, Billie Jean took out her racquet and ball and whacked the ball over and over against the redwood fence in her backyard. Before long the neighbors were complaining about the noise. But eventually they stopped complaining because Billie Jean had practiced so hard and so often that the fence fell apart. Then when Billie Jean was 12, she started taking tennis lessons in a public park in Long Beach from Clyde Walker, a retired tennis player. Walker was Billie's coach and friend until his death in 1961, shortly after Moffitt's first Wimbledon victory.

Billie's enthusiasm for tennis also received an extra boost from a neighbor down the block. The Reverend Bob Richards, the minister of the Moffitt's church, had built his own pole-vaulting pit. In the little free time he had, he practiced tirelessly. In 1952 and 1956 Richards won the Olympic gold medal in pole vaulting. Billie Jean never forgot the example set by the hard-working Bob Richards.

In 1958 Moffitt won her first tennis title, the Southern California Junior Championship for 15 year olds. Even though she was a stocky 5 feet, 4 inches (she later grew two more inches), Moffitt moved quickly over the court and seldom lost a game. The next year at the national championships, Billie battled Maria Bueno from Brazil, winner of the women's singles at Wimbledon and the U.S. Open that year. Shortly after losing to Maria, Moffitt began taking tennis lessons from Alice Marble. Marble was the American star who had won the U.S. Open in 1936, 1938, 1939, and 1940 and at Wimbledon in 1939.

In 1961 Billie, a high school senior, played in her first Wimbledon tournament. She lost her first singles match, but she and her partner, Karen Hantze from San Diego, scored an upset in the women's doubles and became the youngest pair ever to win at Wimbledon. They won the Wimbledon doubles again the following year, and Karen Hantze Susman also won the women's singles title. Billie had beaten top-seeded Margaret Smith Court, 1-6, 6-3, 7-5, in her first round of play but had lost in the quarter-finals. Although Moffitt was beating some of the world's top tennis players in other matches, she was to have three more disappointing years before her first singles victory at Wimbledon.

After high school, Billie had enrolled at Los Angeles State University because she did not think of tennis as a career. There she met Larry King. He helped Billie Jean realize she could become a tennis star if she would work at it full time. King encouraged her to get the kind of serious training she needed to become a winner. Soon after Larry and Billie became engaged, Billie Jean went to Australia to train with Mervyn Rose. Rose had been the men's doubles winner in the 1952 U.S. Open and at Wimbledon in 1954.

In 1965 Billie Jean returned to the courts, determined to win. Shortly before her marriage to King, Billie lost the U.S. Open to Margaret Smith, 6-8, 5-7, but that year she lost no matches to American players.

Starting in 1966, King won three straight Wimbledon singles titles. That year Billie Jean defeated

In the 1966 Wimbledon finals, Billie Jean King played Maria Bueno from Brazil, who had won the singles title three times before.

her old opponents, Margaret Smith (in the semi-finals) and Maria Bueno, 6-3, 3-6, 6-1, (in the finals). In 1967 Billie not only won the women's singles, she also won the women's doubles with partner Rosemary Casals and the mixed doubles (teams of one woman and one man) with Owen Davidson. Winning all three—the singles, the doubles, and the mixed doubles—was winning the Triple Crown. And no one had won the Triple Crown at Wimbledon since 1951. Then King went on to win the Triple Crown at the U.S. Open, too. Winning two triple crowns in the same year was something no one had done for 28 years! For her achievements, King was named the Outstanding Woman Athlete of 1967 and was ranked as the Number One player in the world.

Twenty-four-year-old King turned pro in 1968 when pros were first allowed to play at Wimbledon. That year she again won at Wimbledon, but she lost to Virginia Wade in the finals at the U.S. Open. In 1969 King had a disappointing year and, following knee surgery, lost both Wimbledon and the U.S. Open.

While continuing to be a first-rate player, Billie Jean was becoming more and more interested in what was happening in the business side of tennis. When the officials for the 1970 Pacific Southwest Open refused to pay women winners as much as the men—men would earn $12,000, but women only

$1,500—Billie helped to organize a boycott of the major tennis tournaments. For their activities, King and eight other players were suspended by the United States Lawn Tennis Association (USLTA) and forbidden to enter any USLTA-sponsored tournaments. King then helped to organize a rival tennis association, the Women's International Tennis Federation (WIFT), and the Virginia Slims Tournament. That tournament helped to bring women players better wages for tournament play. That same year, 1970, King again lost to Margaret Smith Court in the longest match in Wimbledon history—two and one-half hours. Shortly afterwards, she had another operation on her knee.

In 1971 King earned $117,000 on the pro tennis circuit—more than any other woman athlete in history or any male tennis player. While she won 19 tournaments that year, Billie lost again at Wimbledon in the semi-finals. Evonne Goolagong went on to win the finals and was named the Number One player. In the U.S. Open, however, King beat Rosemary Casals in the finals 6-4, 7-6.

When the 28-year-old King again faced Goolagong at Wimbledon in the 1972 finals, the tables were turned, and King defeated her, 6-3, 6-3. She also defeated Kerry Melville, 6-3, 7-5, in the U.S. Open and won the French Open. Again she was named the Number One player.

As King continued to win, many urged her to take up the challenge of 55-year-old Bobby Riggs. So after winning the 1973 singles title at Wimbledon from Chris Evert, 6-0, 7-5, King finally agreed to play Riggs. The match was set for September 20, 1973, at the Houston Astrodome.

King knew Riggs' loud boasting and outrageous comments and the television publicity would turn the match into a circus. But she decided she would somehow find a way to concentrate on playing a winning game. In preparing for the match, King knew her poor eyesight would be a disadvantage against Riggs' high lobs. So she practiced hitting such lobs with the bright lights of the Houston Astrodome shining in her eyes. She even watched films of Riggs playing and counted how long it took for his shots to come down.

When the big moment came, Riggs, who had beaten Margaret Court four months earlier, went into his bag of tricks early. He sent up an arching lob at King. King waited calmly and smashed a winner back so hard that Riggs barely had time to move. After that, it was no contest. King won three straight sets, 6-4, 6-3, 6-3, and tennis was never the same again.

The King-Riggs match spurred many people into giving tennis a try. And many more people also became interested in watching professional tennis.

King returns a shot to Bobby Riggs during their well-publicized "battle of the sexes" in 1973.

But the biggest benefit was that more money started flowing into tennis. Organizers were now willing to pay more than ever before to have Billie Jean at their tournaments. King had finally won her case, and she proudly watched as women's prizes began to equal those of men.

The next year, 1974, King helped to organize the World Team Tennis League. She continued to play in tournaments, and she also coached team tennis. Although the top-seeded player at Wimbledon in 1974, King had lost the quarter-finals to Russia's Olga Morozova. But she had gone on to win the mixed doubles with Owen Davidson for her

41

18th Wimbledon title. That year she also won the U.S. Open, 3-6, 6-3, 7-5, against Evonne Goolagong.

At Wimbledon in 1975, Billie played in her ninth finals game. In an exciting comeback, she won the singles for the sixth time for her 19th Wimbledon title. After beating Olga Morozova in the quarter-finals and Chris Evert in the semi-finals, she topped Evonne Goolagong Cawley in the finals, 6-0, 6-1, in only 39 minutes. Afterwards King announced her retirement from the pro circuit.

King did not stay away from pro tennis, however. Although she missed the women's singles at Wimbledon in 1976, she played in the doubles and the mixed doubles that year and in all three competitions from 1977 to 1979. In 1979, after an operation for a foot injury, King earned a record 20th win at Wimbledon when she teamed with Martina Navratilova to capture the women's doubles title.

For all of her talents, Billie Jean King was best known for her eagerness to battle to the end. Not even surgery on both knees kept her from competing, and she was always at her best when the stakes were the highest. And as much as people admired her as a top-notch player, they were even more grateful to her for what she did for the game of tennis. Billie Jean King brought money to tennis, and today all players, both men and women, are enjoying the benefits of her efforts.

5
Chris Evert Lloyd

If someone were making up a story about women tennis players, one could come up with some interesting characters. One person could be a shy, pretty teenager, the favorite of the fans, who battled against older players. Another character could be the cool, calculating veteran who hardly seemed human as she played a "dull," even game of hitting every ball back over the net. People would call her a machine, and she would be the villain of the story. Then there would be the unbeatable champion who would play so skillfully that everyone would have to admire her. Finally there would be an older tennis player who was past her prime and did not seem to have the same determination to win as she had once showed. Every day she would wonder if she should finally retire from the game. While those four characters might seem like completely different kinds of people, they all have been

After defeating Olga Morazova in the 1974 Wimbledon championship game, Chris Evert joyfully tosses her racquet into the air.

descriptions of Chris Evert Lloyd at different times in her career.

Christine Marie Evert was born in Fort Lauderdale, Florida, on December 21, 1954. Her father, John Evert, had spent most of his life working at tennis. After his playing days at Notre Dame University were over, he made a living as a tennis instructor. Chris and the other members of her family sometimes tagged along when Mr. Evert went off to the courts. At the age of six, she began hitting tennis balls around.

John Evert did not want to push his five children into playing high-level tennis. He stressed that the game was meant to be fun. Even when Chris began winning titles, her father would become so nervous that he found little pleasure in watching her compete. Still he acted as her manager.

Chris, however, found fun in competition. The many hours she put into tennis practice did not seem like work to her. Along with her younger sister, Jeanne, she would practice four hours a day on weekdays and as many as nine hours a day on weekends. When Mr. Evert saw that his daughters were really serious about tennis, he helped them follow strict rules about what to eat and how much sleep to get.

When she was in the eighth grade, Chris wanted to be a cheerleader. But she knew that cheerleading would take up much of her time. So Chris finally decided to give up the popular world of cheerleading for the lonely world of tennis.

Right from the start, Chris played well in junior tournaments. She seemed to do especially well on clay courts, where the ball did not bounce very hard. On clay courts she simply wore out opponents with her deep, well-placed shots.

In 1971 the United States women's team needed one more player for their Wightman Cup match with Great Britain. The team organizers had heard that Chris could play well on clay courts. Although she was only 16 years old, Chris was named to play in the tournament. She won, and her fame grew.

Within a few months, Chris was beating top women players, including Great Britain's Virginia Wade and Margaret Court from Australia. That year Evert, a high school junior, fought her way into the semi-finals of the U.S. Open by defeating Leslie Hunt of Australia, 4-6, 6-2, 6-3, in the quarter-finals. At the Open, veteran Billie Jean King showed the teenager she still had a few things to learn and beat her, 6-3, 6-2, in two straight sets. A few months later at another tournament, however, Evert thrashed King, 6-1, 6-0.

During her first few years in the tennis circuit, Chris did not win the important Wimbledon and U.S. Open matches, but she always placed high.

In 1972 at Wimbledon, Evert lost to Evonne Goolagong in the semi-finals of the women's singles, and she lost to Kerry Melville in the semi-finals at the U.S. Open.

In 1972 when she was 18, Chris turned pro. When she decided to play for the USLTA circuit instead of Billie Jean King's newly formed Women's International Tennis Federation, her choice caused some hard feelings from some of the older players. But Evert defended her decision by saying she wanted the chance to participate in the major USLTA-sponsored tournaments, such as Wimbledon and the U.S. Open. She felt that the older players, including King and Court, had already had their chance to play in these tournaments, and now she wanted hers. It was not until 1974, when the two pro tours merged, that Chris would face all of the game's top women players.

In 1973 Evert lost the French Open to Margaret Court, but she then defeated Court, 6-1, 1-6, 6-1, in the semi-finals at Wimbledon. When Evert lost to King in the Wimbledon finals, it had been the first time since 1957 that two Americans had played in the final game of women's singles. Evert again lost to Court in the semi-finals of the U.S. Open. That was her third straight loss in the Open semi-finals.

Despite her losses, tennis followers were keeping their eyes on Chris. People especially noticed

At her first U.S. Open appearance in 1972, Chris Evert showed her famous two-handed backhand shot.

her unusual two-handed backhand. Most experts believed that having both hands on the racquet would shorten a player's reach. But Chris insisted that she could not get enough power *without* using two hands, and her two-fisted backhands would shoot across the net as fast as her forehand. Because of her popularity, Chris had problems with some of the other players, who could not help but feel envious of the youngster who was on her way to earning a million dollars before her 21st birthday.

By 1974 when Chris' wins were becoming frequent, she was no longer the darling little girl whom everyone was rooting for. The British newspeople, especially, turned on her. They found Evert's tactic of wearing down her opponents boring. Chris rarely rushed the net, and her opponents were leery of wandering too close to the net because Evert was an expert at beating such tactics with well-placed passing shots down the sidelines. The result was that Chris simply traded shots with her opponents until they would make a mistake. Critics called her a lifeless ball-returning machine. To many, Evert seemed too cool and too professional. She never showed emotion, never seemed to work up a sweat. Because of her constant, serious concentration, some people called her "Ice Princess."

In 1974 Evert beat Martina Navratilova in the Italian Open and Olga Morozova at the French Open. With Morozova, she also won the women's doubles at both tournaments. That year at Wimbledon, Evert again defeated Morozova, 6-0, 6-4, in the finals for her 36th victory in a row. That same year, her fiance, Jimmy Connors, had defeated Ken Rosewall in the men's finals, so it was a double victory for the United States' two Number One players. Later Connors and Evert decided not to marry, and they broke off their engagement.

In 1975 when Chris was named Female Athlete of the Year for the second straight year, she lost the Wimbledon finals to Billie Jean King. But she

Evert won her second Wimbledon singles title by defeating Evonne Goolagong in 1976.

won the U.S. Open, 5-7, 6-4, 6-2, against Evonne Goolagong. Evert had gone into the finals with a record of 83 straight match wins.

Evert again won against Goolagong in the 1976 Wimbledon finals, 6-3, 4-5, 8-6, and she beat Evonne in the U.S. Open, 6-3, 6-0. She also won the U.S. Open against Wendy Turnbull of Australia, 7-6, 6-2, in 1977 and against Pam Shriver, 7-5, 6-4, in 1978.

There was nothing like success to stop the earlier criticism of Chris Evert, however, and as she continued to be the world's top-ranked woman tennis player, criticism turned to praise and recognition for her achievements. During those years, there were stretches when Chris simply overmatched even the best of her opponents. From 1973 to 1978, she was a killer on clay courts, and she had won 125 straight matches on clay before losing to Tracy Austin in the semi-finals of the 1979 Italian Open. For her fine playing, Chris was named the Female Athlete of the Year by the Associated Press (AP) in 1974, 1975, 1977. Besides earning a fortune in prize money, she won enough cars to start her own dealership.

But in 1979 Chris Evert seemed to be just a poor imitation of the old Chris. She was losing more often, and she suffered some embarrassingly one-sided defeats against Tracy Austin. On the court Evert looked tired and listless, as if she were getting tired of the whole game. That year Chris took off time for other activities, including an April marriage to John Lloyd, a popular British tennis star. After her marriage, she even announced that she was through with tennis, and she did leave the game for three months.

Then in 1980 Chris seemed to come alive again. She reeled off another of the famous Evert streaks, winning 26 straight matches. At Wimbledon she

Chris Evert Lloyd was jubliant after winning her fifth
U.S. Open title in 1980.

beat the defending champion, Martina Navratilova,
and zipped into the finals against Evonne Goolagong.
In the finals, Evert played well but was defeated in
her only tournament loss that year after 40 wins.
Then at the U.S. Open, Chris beat Andrea Jaeger in
the quarter-finals and Tracy Austin in the semi-

finals, 4-6, 6-1, 6-1, and finally topped Hana Mandlikova, 5-7, 6-1, 6-1, in the finals for her fifth U.S. Open title.

To top off the year, Chris regained her Number One ranking from the Women's Tennis Association and was again named the AP's Female Athlete of the Year. People realized, at age 26, the "old" Chris Evert was still one of the game's most popular players. And Lloyd's wins continued in 1981 when she won her third Wimbledon singles title by defeating Hana Mandlikova, 6-2, 6-2, in only 60 minutes. Although Mandlikova had defeated Lloyd several weeks earlier in the French Open and had won both the French and the Australian opens, it was a nervous Hana who was playing in her first Wimbledon finals against the veteran Lloyd in her seventh finals game. (A pregnant Evonne Goolagong, the 1980 Wimbledon winner, did not compete.)

As new young favorites such as Tracy Austin, Pam Shriver, and Andrea Jaeger, arrived on the tennis scene, Chris went out of her way to treat them well. She remembered what it had been like when she had been trying to be accepted by the older players. In many ways, she had paved the way for those younger players. And as they received more and more attention, it is unlikely that they would ever face quite the attention that Evert had during her ever-changing career.

In her first Wimbledon contest in 1971, Evonne Goolagong faced three-time Wimbledon champion, Margaret Court—and won.

6
Evonne Goolagong Cawley

Ken and Melina Goolagong lived in Barellan, Australia, a small town of about 900 people, 360 miles from Sydney. The Goolagongs—whose name meant "tall trees by still waters"—were the only Aborigines there. Aborigines were dark-skinned people who lived in Australia long before European settlers arrived. Ken Goolagong made a meager living by shearing sheep. The Goolagong family was probably among the poorest in that hot, dusty town on the edge of Australia's sheep country.

In 1951 Ken Goolagong bought an old second-hand car. While cleaning out the back seat, he came across some dirty tennis balls. He cleaned them up and gave them to the newborn Goolagong baby, Evonne, to play with. For years Evonne would carry those tennis balls around with her wherever she went. Perhaps it was an early sign that this third of the eight Goolagong children was going to grow up to become one of the world's best tennis players.

As a child, Evonne liked to play rough games, such as rugby. She also enjoyed running. Goolagong was a natural athlete with a graceful stride and quick reflexes. She was also a quick learner.

Evonne started going to the tennis courts in Barellan when she was 5, and at the age of 6, she received her first racquet from an aunt. Evonne seemed a natural tennis player. After winning some local championships, Evonne drew the attention of Victor Edwards, a well-known tennis instructor from Sydney. Edwards convinced the Goolagongs to let their 13-year-old daughter live with his family. Then she could get the competition and practice she would need to become a successful tennis player. The people in Barellan were as excited for Evonne as her family was, and they chipped in almost $1,000 to help support Evonne in her career.

It was not easy for a 13-year old to leave her family, and Evonne was nervous about coming to the big city. But Evonne soon found out that some people in Sydney were just as nervous about her. When some people heard that Evonne was an Aborigine, they pictured some wild bush woman carrying a spear! But it did not take long before Evonne and her hosts grew comfortable with each other.

While living in Sydney, Evonne was under a strict

training program, and her skills improved tremendously. By the time she was 18, she had won more than 80 tournaments. In 1970 when she was 19, her coach sent her overseas so she could gain experience by playing against the world's best players. But long before anyone had expected her to, Evonne started beating those she was supposed to be learning from! That year she advanced to the second round at Wimbledon. Although she lost the Australian Open a few weeks later, she went on to win the Victoria State Championship in Melbourne in a 7-6, 7-6 upset game.

Then in 1971 Evonne won the French Open by defeating 27-year-old Margaret Smith Court, 7-6, 7-6. Court had always been Evonne's idol. Next Evonne surprised everyone, including her coach, by making it into the finals at Wimbledon. People had figured she was at least a few years away from being a champion.

Evonne's opponent in the Wimbledon finals that year was Margaret Court, who had won the women's singles at Wimbledon the year before. So although Goolagong had defeated Court before, no one was more surprised than Goolagong when she easily won the championship from her, 6-4, 6-1, in only 63 minutes. (In the semi-finals Goolagong had defeated Billie Jean King, 6-4, 6-4.)

Tennis experts agreed that they had never seen

such a smooth, graceful player as Goolagong. And her carefree attitude was also rare in the pressure-filled world of sports. That year Evonne was named the world's top woman athlete.

At Wimbledon in 1972, Goolagong beat Chris Evert, 4-6, 6-3, 6-4, in the semi-finals, but she lost to 28-year-old Billie Jean King in the finals.

The following year, 1973, was not a winning one for Goolagong. While she won the Italian Open from Evert and the Canadian Open, she lost to her rival, Margaret Court, in the Australian Open, in the semi-finals of the French Open, and in the finals of the U.S. Open. That year she also lost to King in semi-final play at Wimbledon.

Evonne, however, was the kind of player who could smile at her bad shots. In fact, she would smile most of the time she was on the court. She seemed to enjoy running after shots. At the start of her career, reporters tried to build her up as the rival of Chris Evert. But Evonne was not one for rivalries. She played tennis because it was fun. If she lost, she would forget about it, and later she would often go off and enjoy herself at a dance.

Goolagong's attitude also carried over to the financial side of pro tennis. In an age where athletes often kept one eye out for business deals and investments, Goolagong seemed different. After winning one tournament, Evonne was mistakenly given the check meant for a much lower finisher. If a friend had not pointed out the mistake, Goolagong would never have noticed!

Goolagong's carefree spirit, however, could also sometimes cause her problems in competition. If an opponent played badly, Evonne would often lose interest in the game and would start to play as poorly as her opponent. There was also something her coach called the "Goolagong fog." Many times Evonne would completely overwhelm an opponent at the start of a match. Then all of a sudden she would seem to forget everything she had ever learned about the game. It was as if she would quit paying attention to what she was doing.

Once in the middle of a match, Evonne seemed to go into her deep fog for several games. But just as suddenly as she had lost her touch, she would regain it and would win the match. When asked what had happened, Evonne would claim she had been trying to remember a tune she had heard. Then when the tune had finally come to her, she would go back to playing her best tennis!

Evonne's attitude and personality made her one of the most unpredictable players in tennis. Often she would sail past the toughest of rivals but then would turn around and lose to some unknown player. But when she was at her best, there was no stopping Goolagong from winning.

In 1974 Evonne won the Italian Open against Billie Jean King and the French Open against Chris Evert without losing a set in either tournament. That year she also defeated Chris Evert at the Australian Open. While she lost in the quarter-finals at Wimbledon, she and her partner, Peggy Michel, won the doubles. Then she beat Chris Evert in the semi-finals at the U.S. Open, 6-0, 6-7, 6-3, to end Evert's 52-game winning streak, but she lost to King in the finals. She also lost to King in the 1975 Wimbledon finals.

In 1977 Evonne married Roger Cawley from England, and the tennis world heard little about Evonne. She and Roger had moved to Hilton Head, South Carolina, and were raising a baby girl, Kelly Irala. (In Aborigine, Irala means, "a peaceful place.")

Then in 1980 Evonne was back on the courts. But it soon was obvious that nagging injuries and illness were slowing her down. By the time the 1980 Wimbledon tournament came around, Evonne had not won a single tournament. But Wimbledon that year was a turning point for Goolagong. In a qualifying match, Evonne upset the marvelous teenager, Tracy Austin, to earn a spot in the finals.

In the finals, Evonne again found herself facing Chris Evert Lloyd. Nine years earlier, Evonne had stood at the same net and had beaten Margaret Court. Could she win after such a long time?

Evonne Goolagong Cawley slams a return to Chris Evert Lloyd during their 1980 championship match at Wimbledon.

When the match began, Evonne proved to be in rare form. Although the skies were cloudy and the match was interrupted by rain, there was no Goolagong fog that day. Instead she won the title, 6-1, 7-6. The smiling, graceful tennis star had come back, and it was easy to tell by the crowd's cheers that they were glad to welcome her.

A pleased Evonne Cawley holds her Wimbledon trophy after her 1980 comeback win.

7
Martina Navratilova

Martina Navratilova saw the United States for the first time in 1973. To the 16-year old from Czechoslovakia, it seemed like a dream land. She loved the shops, the food, the entertainment, and all of the modern conveniences. Two years later, when she made her home in that fascinating new country, she was unaware that her dream land would soon turn into a nightmare.

Martina was born in Czechoslovakia on October 18, 1956. From an early age, Martina was a splendid athlete, and she enjoyed skiing, soccer, and tennis. Like her grandmother, who had been a highly-ranked tennis player in Czechoslovakia before World War II, Martina became a fierce competitor on the courts. Martina was only eight years old when she entered her first tennis tournament, and she advanced to the semi-finals before losing.

Martina Navratilova returned to Wimbledon in 1979 to defend the title she had won from Chris Evert the previous year.

In her home country, Martina moved quickly through the top ranks of girls' tennis. She became such a fine player that in 1973, at the age of 16, she was allowed to compete in tournaments throughout the world. The contacts she made with other top players gave Martina the experience she needed to develop her raw talent. By 1974 Martina had risen from an unknown teenager to one of the world's most respected women tennis players.

In 1975 Martina just missed winning the Australian, the Italian, and the French opens, losing each in the final round. But after her performances, tennis experts everywhere remarked that Martina had the ability to become a first-rate tennis player. But they also agreed that Martina would have to overcome some problems in order to reach the top.

Most experts felt that Martina's biggest problem was her concentration, which seemed to depend on her mood. Like Evonne Goolagong, Martina could be brilliant one day and ordinary the next. Some also thought that Navratilova did not practice enough, and others felt that Martina's aggressive nature was causing her to make mistakes in her game.

In 1975 when everyone was becoming excited about Martina's potential, Navratilova returned from a United States tennis tour and announced that she was defecting to the States. Life in Czechoslovakia had never been easy. In 1968 the Soviet Union, angered about Czechoslovakia's falling away from the true communistic principles, had sent their tanks and troops into Czechoslovakia. Then Martina had been 11 years old, and she had seen Russian troops storming her hometown. Terrified, she had run into a store and had hidden there for hours. Her father finally found her and took her home, but Martina had never forgotten that terrible incident.

Although the United States seemed like a good place to live, it was not an easy decision for Navratilova to leave her home. She would have to leave her parents and sister behind, and life for them as relatives of a defector would be unpleasant. Many said Martina was making an irresponsible choice, and they claimed she was just wasting her life and spoiling herself with American riches. They felt the proof was in the 40 pounds she had gained while she had been in the United States.

Beginning a new life in the United States would have been hard enough for Martina without such criticism. For when she moved to the States, she was all alone without any family or friends. One day while driving near her new home in Dallas, Texas, Martina found a stray dog wandering on the freeway. Because the dog also seemed to be lonely and without a real home—as she felt she was— Martina took the dog home for companionship.

As might have been expected, Martina's loneliness

seemed to affect her tennis game. After leaving Czechoslovakia, Navratilova played tennis for 11 months without winning a single tournament. The worst moment of all for Martina came at the 1975 U.S. Open. Martina was expected to easily polish off a young player named Janet Newberry in the first round of the tournament. As expected, she breezed through the first set, winning 6-1. After that, however, she lost control of the match. Martina seemed helpless as Newberry closed out the match with 6-4, 6-4 victories in the final set.

When the match was over, Martina stood on the court in shock. As the crowd watched in stunned silence, she broke down and sobbed hysterically. Newberry finally helped her to the dressing room.

A turning point came for Martina when she met Sandra Haynie. Haynie, a professional golfer, had won the U.S. Open in golf in 1974. Sandra knew the kind of pressure Martina was facing, and she did her best to help her. The two soon became friends and then roommates. Navratilova took it easy for a while and played in fewer tournaments. Instead she worked on improving her tennis game and on getting herself into shape.

Avoiding reporters, Martina returned in full force to the court in 1978. At 5 feet, 7 inches, and 132 pounds, Navratilova was again the picture of perfect health, and the 21-year old also had some surprises for the tennis world. Somehow Martina seemed to have gained what she had always been missing— total concentration. No longer did she give away points on careless mistakes. And her serve was stronger than ever. Martina was blasting her left-handed serve at a speed of more than 90 miles per hour, the fastest in women's tennis! Martina's big serve would often put her foe on the defensive. And when it did, Martina would rush to the net and put away the weak return of her receiver.

In the first year of her comeback, 1978, Navratilova met Chris Evert, the world's top woman player, in the finals at Wimbledon. In a hard-fought, three-set game, Navratilova came away with the trophy, 6-4, 4-6, 9-7. Even though she later lost to American Pam Shriver in the U.S. Open semi-finals, Martina was ranked as the Number One player by the Women's Tennis Association that year.

Although Martina was now winning most of her matches, one thing was still upsetting her. Newspapers and radios in Czechoslovakia refused to report any news about Martina. Although they had tried many times, her family had never been able to get government permission to see one of her tournaments. Martina tried to make up for the lack of contact with telephone calls. She ran up bills of $200 a call, but telephoning was just not the same as seeing her family in person.

Navratilova leaps high to return a shot in her 1978 Wimbledon finals game with Chris Evert.

Martina proudly hoists her second Wimbledon trophy.

In 1979 Martina's mother was finally able to see her daughter play when she was given permission to visit England for the Wimbledon tournament. There Martina made certain her mother saw her at her best. Navratilova faced Evert in the finals, and again she won easily, 6-4, 6-4. It was performances like Wimbledon that helped Martina win the Number

One ranking in women's tennis that year from the United States Tennis Association.

Martina, however, had troubles again at the U.S. Open in 1979, and she lost in the semi-finals to Tracy Austin. The next year, 1980, Martina was the second-seeded woman player at the U.S. Open, but she lost her quarter-final game to 18-year-old Hana Mandlikova, another Czech player. (Mandlikova would later lose to Evert in the finals.) Despite her losses, she was still ranked third by both the U.S. Tennis Association and the Women's Tennis Association. In 1980 Navratilova also became a U.S. citizen.

After some terrible pressures, Martina had seemed to have adjusted remarkably well to American life and to being a winning player. She loved to win at card games, too, and she could put on some clever moves playing one-to-one basketball. After only four years in the United States, Martina, the tennis star, was nearly as unbeatable in English word games as she was on the tennis courts!

8
Tracy Austin

For a 16-year-old girl to win the U.S. Open tennis title would ordinarily be a huge shock. But by her 16th birthday, Tracy Austin had already become a familiar name in tennis. People had been saying for years that someday she would be one of the best. No other tennis player had ever shown such obvious ability at an early age as Tracy Austin had.

Tracy, who was born on December 12, 1962, in Rolling Hills, California, seemed to have been destined for fame. Before she was born, Tracy's mother had taken up tennis as part of an exercise program, and soon the whole family was playing tennis. By the time Tracy came along, there were already six Austins battling for honors on the tennis courts, including Tracy's older sister, Pam, and her three older brothers, Jeff, Doug, and John.

By the age of three, little Tracy Austin already knew how to swing a tennis racquet.

Tracy, the youngest child, was not one to be left out of the family pastime. By the age of three, she was toddling around the courts, dragging a sawed-off tennis racquet behind her. The racquet was not just for show either. Tracy had started taking lessons at the age of two, so she could already bat the ball around.

When she was just four years old, Tracy's picture had been splashed across newspapers and magazines around the world. Publications such as *World Tennis* thought it a cute tribute to a tennis family to put a picture of the youngest member on the cover.

Nine years later, Tracy was back on magazine covers. But that time it was for something more than just being a cute kid. Experts usually hated to predict stardom for a child because so much could happen by the time she or he had grown up. But in 1976 some of the smartest people in tennis were saying that 13-year-old Tracy Austin would be the next Chris Evert. Not too many people, however, were surprised by that prediction because Tracy, who had entered her first tennis tournament at the age of 7, had already beaten the best of the older girls. At the age of 11, she had won the national title for 12-year-old girls. And when she was 12 and again at 13, Tracy had won the 14-year-old title. At age 13, she had been the top-ranked player among girls 14 and under, and she had never lost a match in her own age group.

Tracy was the most advanced girl in the history of tennis. The pros who had been hired to teach her had to think hard to earn their money because there was very little about tennis that she did not already know. They all agreed, however, that Tracy did need to work on her serve. Tracy needed to come up with a more powerful serve—one that would drive her opponents away from the nets so that she would have a more open court to aim at.

Tracy worked hard to develop a strong first serve and soon became better than ever. In 1977 after 14-year-old Tracy had won the 18-year-old championship, she was invited to play in the 100th anniversary Wimbledon tournament—the youngest person to play in that famous tournament in 90 years. Although she lost to Chris Evert in the quarter-finals, 6-1, 6-1, young Austin delighted the British crowd. They marveled at how a girl 3 inches shorter than 5 feet could trade shots with a fully-grown woman. Along with her size, Tracy's pigtails, pin-afores, and the braces on her teeth made her look even more like a small child.

Throughout her Wimbledon matches, the normally calm British crowds cheered Tracy's every move. Her opponents, however, did not find it so amusing. Beating little Tracy looked much easier than it really was. Players who had spent their whole lives trying to win respect as top competitors were embarrassed to be beaten by such a tiny foe.

That year in the U.S. Open, Tracy made it into the semi-finals before losing, just as Chris Evert had done when she had been 16. Afterwards she joined the Virginia Slims tournament, but because she was still an amateur, 14-year-old Tracy could not keep any of her winnings.

Austin's opponents were finding that her style could often make the most experienced player look bad. Tracy would be content just to hit the ball back and then to wait for the other person to make a mistake. Her patience was almost maddening to her opponents. Playing against Austin was like playing against a wall. Every shot a player would hit at Tracy would come right back! After awhile even the most experienced player would lose patience and would try to end the game with a risky shot. Often she would miss the shot. But even if Tracy's opponent would put the shot into Austin's court, Tracy would somehow be able to return the ball and then would wait for another mistake.

In 1977 and 1978 Tracy did not win any major tournaments, but she beat many of the top players. In 1978 when she was almost 16, Tracy, now 5 feet, 4 inches, and 110 pounds, joined the pros. In her first three months as a pro, Austin won three tournaments. It seemed as though all of the old predictions about her success were coming true.

In 1979 Tracy defeated veteran Billie Jean King, the winner of 19 Wimbledon titles, in the Wimbledon quarter-finals before losing to two-time Wimbledon singles winner, Martina Navratilova, in the semi-finals. One of Austin's most exciting wins that year was in her U.S. Open semi-finals game against Martina. Navratilova had gone into her match with Austin hoping to add to her 37-game winning streak. But when the match was over, Martina went away muttering instead. Tracy's patient play had worn her down, and she had defeated her, 7-5, 7-5.

In the finals game, Tracy's opponent was 24-year-old Chris Evert Lloyd, the world's top tennis player. As the match started, Chris may have been thinking about her early years in the game when the crowds had been on her side. Now the cheers were for Tracy instead.

Austin and Lloyd played the same kind of game. Both stubbornly slugged away with their best shots from deep in their own courts. During one rally, the ball crossed the net 50 times before one of them won the point! In the end, Tracy outlasted Chris, 6-4, 6-3, to become the youngest woman ever to win the U.S. Open. (Evert and Goolagong had won when they were 19, and Maureen Connolly had been 17 when she had won in 1952.) That year Austin had already ended Lloyd's 125-match winning streak on clay courts when she had defeated her in the semi-finals of the Italian Open.

Despite her winning, it was still hard to think of the pig-tailed Tracy as anything but a little girl. Even the defeated Lloyd had congratulated her by absent-mindedly patting her on the head!

Tracy Austin jumps for joy after defeating Chris Evert Lloyd in the finals of the 1979 U.S. Open.

The next year at Wimbledon, Tracy made it all the way to the semi-finals, but was beaten in that game by Evonne Goolagong, 6-3, 0-6, 6-4. Then at the U.S. Open, 17-year-old Austin, the top-seeded woman player, beat 18-year-old Pam Shriver, 6-2, 6-3, in the quarter-finals. But the tables were turned when Tracy was beaten in the semi-finals. Although Tracy had defeated Chris Evert Lloyd in the Open the year before and had been the winner in their five previous matches, she lost to Lloyd, 6-4, 1-6, 1-6. In 1980 in the U.S. Tennis Association ratings, Tracy moved from the third place she had held in 1978 and 1979 to first place. She also placed second to Lloyd in Women's Tennis Association rankings and as AP's Female Athlete of the Year.

A proud Tracy poses with her U.S. Open cup.

After every tournament, Austin eagerly returned to her classroom to resume the normal life of a teenager—or as normal a life a top-ranked tennis player could have. She had to devote a great deal of her time to her tennis and was constantly surrounded by reporters wanting interviews. During the pro circuit, she would try to alternate two weeks of school with one week on tour. An "A" student, she worked as hard in school as on the tennis courts.

Tracy's strength on the tennis court continues to be simply knowing how to win. She does not always seem to play better than her opponents, but when it comes to the important points that decide a match, she somehow usually winds up on the top. While she concentrates on winning, Tracy rarely gets upset when she loses. She knows she has played her best and cannot hope to win every match every time she plays.